49574

W9-AHW-641

MISTAKEN JOURNEY

AS TOLD TO BEN EAST

ILLUSTRATED & DESIGNED BY JACK DAHL

EDITED BY JEROLYN NENTL AND DR. HOWARD SCHROEDER

Professor in Reading and Language Arts, Dept. of Elementary Education, Mankato State University

1.50

Library of Congress Cataloging in Publication Data

East, Ben
    Mistaken Journey, as told to Ben East.
    (Survival)
    SUMMARY: A rancher, his family, and two companions journey through 300 miles of rough, unsettled country to the land the family will homestead in Canada only to realize they have been trekking in the wrong direction.
    1. Frontier and pioneer life--British Columbia--Juvenile literature. 2. British Columbia--Description and travel--Juvenile literature. 3. Wilderness survival--British Columbia--Juvenile literature. (1. Wilderness survival. 2. Survival) I. Dahl, John I. II. Nentl, Jerolyn Ann. III. Schroeder, Howard. IV. Title. V. Series.
F1087.4.E17   917.11'2'04   79-53775
ISBN 0-89686-046-9 lib. bdg.
ISBN 0-89686-054-X pbk.

International Standard Book Numbers:	Library of Congress Catalog Number:
0-89686-046-9 Library Bound	
0-89686-054-X Paperback	79-53775

Adapted from the original publication *Danger* by **Outdoor Life,** Copyright 1970.

CRESTWOOD·HOUSE

P.O. Box 3427
Hwy. 66 South
Mankato, MN 56001

ABOUT THE AUTHOR...

Ben East has been an *Outdoor Life* staff editor since 1946. Born in south-eastern Michigan in 1898, and a lifelong resident of that state, he sold his first story to *Outers Recreation* (later absorbed by *Outdoor Life*) in 1921. In 1926 he began a career as a professional writer, becoming outdoor editor of Booth Newspapers, a chain of dailies in eight major Michigan cities outside Detroit.

He left the newspaper job on January 1, 1946, to become Midwest field editor of Outdoor Life. In 1966 he was advanced to senior field editor, a post from which he retired at the end of 1970. Since then he has continued to write for the magazine as a contributing field editor.

Growing up as a farm boy, he began fishing and hunting as soon as he could handle a cane pole and a .22 rifle. He has devoted sixty years to outdoor sports, travel, adventure, wildlife photography, writing and lecturing. Ben has covered much of the back country of North America, from the eastern seaboard to the Aleutian Islands of Alaska, and from the Canadian arctic to the southern United States. He has written more than one thousand magazine articles and eight books. Today his by-line is one of the best known of any outdoor writer in the country. His outstanding achievement in wildlife photography was the making of the first color film ever taken of the Alaskan sea otter, in the summer of 1941.

In recent years much of his writing has dealt with major conservation problems confronting the nation. He has produced hard-hitting and effective articles on such environmentally destructive practices as strip mining, channelization, unethical use of aircraft to take trophy game, political interference in wildlife affairs, the indiscriminate use of pesticides and the damming of wild and scenic rivers and streams.

In 1973, he was signally honored when the Michigan Senate and House of Representatives adopted a concurrent resolution, the legislature's highest tribute, recognizing him for his distinguished contribution to the conservation of natural resources.

A FOREWORD TO MISTAKEN JOURNEY

Eight years after she and her family had made the long, hard trip through the unmapped wilderness, Eunice Neighbor told me this story. I came to know her as a result of another exciting and dangerous experience she and her husband had had.

About three months after the Neighbors completed their move to a new ranch on Cypress Creek, one of the neighbors, who lived eight miles from them was traveling nearby. He was leading an untamed horse behind his saddle horse along a trail. The animal reared, fell, and broke it's neck.

Later a big grizzly bear found the dead horse and began to feed on it. When a grizzly discovers a food supply of that kind, he is not likely to give it up to anything without a fight.

Hersch Neighbor was away from home at the time, with a crew of men fighting a forest fire. His ride home took him past the dead horse. The bear rushed out of the brush, sent Hersch's pack horse into a panic, and gave Hersch a bad scare!

When he finally got home, he and Eunice agreed the grizzly would have to be killed. A band of Indians had camped nearby. If any Indian children should wander near the bear a tragic killing was almost sure to happen.

Hersch, Eunice, and a hired ranch hand went after the bear the next morning. To their surprise, when they got near the place, not one but four grizzlies came at them. There was a large female, and three smaller bears, weighing about two hundred pounds each. They were as angry as the female and big enough to be dangerous.

The attack lasted about five minutes. When it ended the three people had fired ten shots, and all four bears were dead. The three, very shaken, skinned the bears and headed back to their ranch.

After the story of the MISTAKEN JOURNEY appeared in Outdoor Life, I worked with Eunice in putting together the tale of the grizzly ambush. We have never met face to face, but I still count her among my good friends.

BEN EAST

Hersch Neighbor was a rancher in British Columbia, Canada. Ranching was hard work, and the land Hersch and his wife, Eunice, owned was poor. The wild grass was too soft to make good winter feed. Hersch did not mind the hard work. In fact, he liked it. What he did not like was working so hard and getting so little in return. The idea of moving had been on his mind for a long time, but he hated to think of pulling up stakes and leaving. He and his family had put in thirteen years of hard work on their spread at Tete Jaune Cache, seventy miles west of Jasper Park. The fact was becoming more clear each year that they had not chosen a good place to settle.

One day Hersch said to his wife, "We're going to move."

"Where to?" she quickly asked. Her cheerfulness surprised Hersch.

"I didn't expect you'd go for it," he said.

"If it has good grass and good hunting, it'll be better than this," she told him.

Hersch explained that he had been thinking of moving to the Anahim Lake area which was west of their present ranch. When summertime came, Hersch and his wife set out to see if the new area would be good ranch country. Their sixteen-year-old son, Nod, went with them. For three weeks, they explored the area. Just as they had heard, the land was good, but it was all taken. The land that remained for homesteading was too poor for ranching. The disheartened family returned home to make other plans. A friend told them that good grassland could be found along Halfway River. He suggested they also take a look along Cypress Creek, which was north of the Peace River. In October they left home once more to try and find good land to homestead. This time they took their thirteen-year-old daughter, Sandy, with them. The three rode a full day over a pack trail to the Halfway River. Next, they traveled for a day down the river to Cypress Creek. There they found what they had been looking for, wild, virgin country. There was plenty of good hard grass plus a beautiful view of the mountains twelve miles to the west. Living there would mean real pioneering. It would mean more hard work, too. They would be twenty-five miles

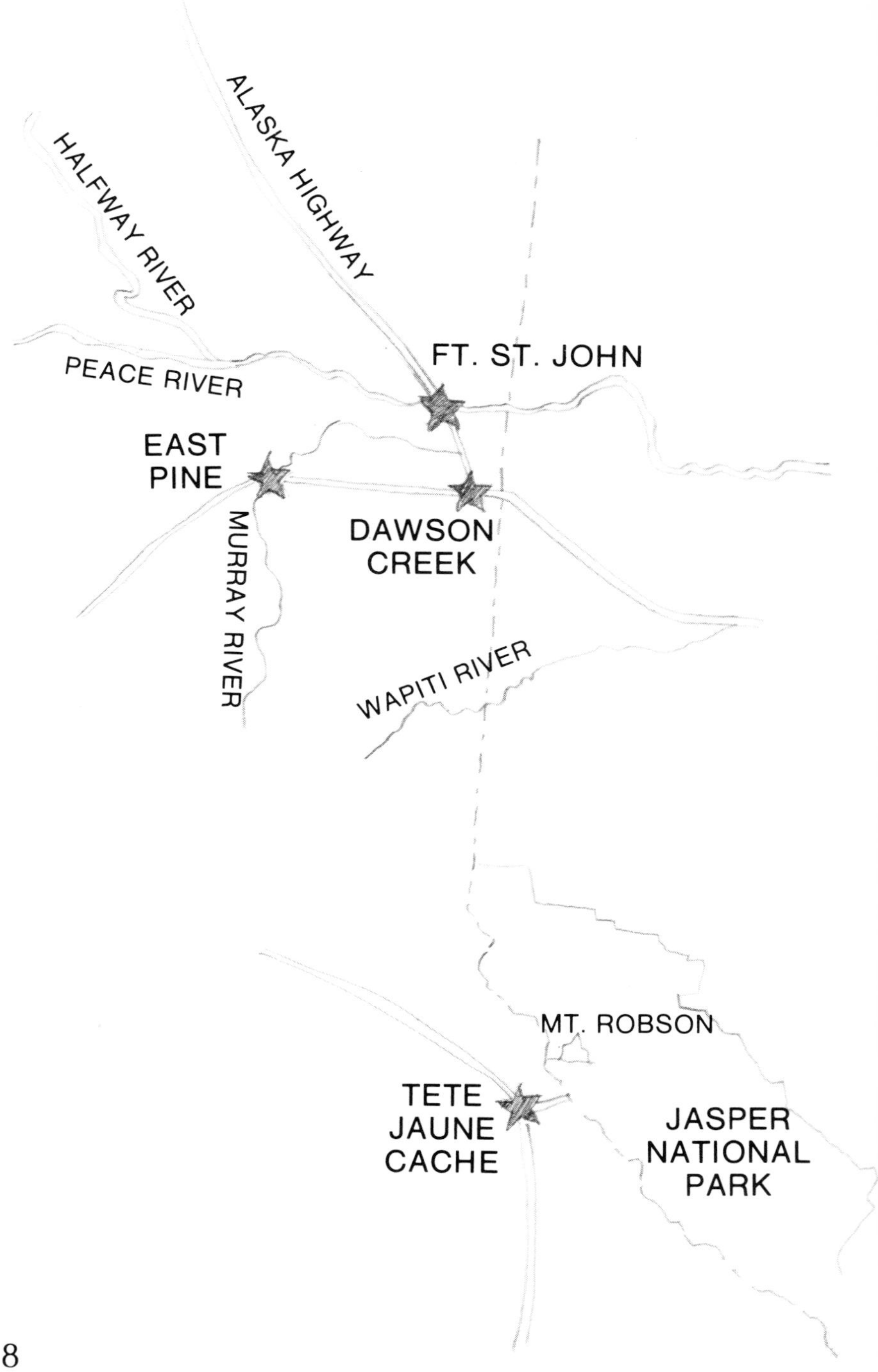

HALFWAY RIVER

ALASKA HIGHWAY

PEACE RIVER

FT. ST. JOHN

EAST
PINE

MURRAY RIVER

DAWSON
CREEK

WAPITI RIVER

MT. ROBSON

TETE
JAUNE
CACHE

JASPER
NATIONAL
PARK

8

from the nearest road, the Alaska Highway. Their only close neighbors would be two men who lived half-a-mile away. Two other men lived eight miles to the south while another lived ten miles to the north. The closest town, Fort St. John, was 123 miles away. To get there, they would have to travel twenty-five miles east to the highway and then ninety-eight miles south. It would be twenty-three miles just to the nearest telephone! Truly, it was wild country, and that is what the Neighbors wanted. Hersch arranged to homestead 320 acres on Cypress Creek.

There were a few problems in moving to such a remote place. First, a cabin had to be built. The Neighbors could truck their household goods along the Alaska Highway, but there remained the twenty-five miles into the bush, which would have to be made by pack horse and wagon. To move his ranch stock, Hersch made other plans. He would trail the horses through the mountains to the Halfway River valley. By going in the fall, he could also do some hunting. After reaching the valley, the horses would be put up for the winter and Hersch would return to the home ranch at Tete Jaune Cache. Once spring came, they would finish the move. The pack trip would cover three hundred miles of rough, unsettled country. They didn't even have maps of the last two hundred miles to be covered.

Such a trip did not worry Hersch and Eunice. They had always felt at home in the wilderness.

Hersch had been born in Oregon. His family had always lived in the hills. They were hunters and stockmen. When Hersch was nine, his family moved to Canada and settled on a bush homestead in Alberta. Hersch went on his first hunting trip when he was seventeen. The next year, he started work as a guide for other hunters. For as long as he could remember, Hersch had loved the mountains and bush country.

Eunice had also been born on a bush homestead in Canada, but left when she was nine to go to school. When she was sixteen, Eunice went back to the bush country and married Hersch. Until then, she had never touched a gun, and knew little about life in the forest.

Hersch was a good teacher, and Eunice learned quickly. In the 1930's, they started a business in central Alberta that offered pack horse and guide service to hunters. At first, all went well and they made a good living at it. Then farmers began settling the land, and building fences around their crops. The fences made Hersch and Eunice feel cramped. They packed up and moved to the Tete Jaune Cache ranch to start again. If they had done it before, they could do it again.

Hersch planned the pack trip with care. He chose a route that would lead into the mountains at Mt. Robson. From there, they would follow the British Columbia and Alberta border to the headwaters of the Murray River. The Murray would lead them to the town of East Pine on the Hart Highway. At that point they would strike out through the woods to the Peace River country. There they would find the Halfway River and follow it to Cypress Creek. The trip would take about thirty days. They would be in familiar territory until they got to Kakwa Lake. Once they left the lake, the country would be all new to them.

Sandy and Nod would go along with their parents. Sandy was now fourteen and had finished the eighth grade. Nod was seventeen and showed little interest in horses or in riding them, but had a good sense of humor and was eager to learn. He would be a good one to have along for the trip.

Two other people were also going along. One was Art Mintz, a young man the Neighbors had known since he was nine. He had worked for them for the last few years. His father was a logger and a trapper, and Art had grown up in the bush country. He worried a lot, but had a sharp sense of humor and met each hardship with a grin and smart remark. Art would be a good addition to the group. Jim Scott, who had been a rancher in Montana, would

also go with them. Hersch and Eunice met Jim when they had done guide and pack work for him on hunting trips. Jim wanted to go on this trip so he could hunt. His goal was to get good head trophies of all the big game in that part of the country.

On a beautiful August day, Hersch led them, plus sixteen pack horses, away from the home ranch. The trees were yellowing, but the leaves had not started to fall. Autumn was at hand, and they knew there might be bad weather in the mountains. However, the Neighbors were eager and were looking for a new life, not just a trail ride.

They rode the nineteen miles to Mt. Robson, unpacked and fed the horses. By the time they had pitched their tents and sat down to supper, it was seven p.m. The camp, with its three tents, was cozy and cheerful. The tent that Sandy was to sleep in was also used for cooking and eating. Nod, Art, and Jim would share a smaller tent. Hersch and Eunice used a reflector type tent that looked like a lean-to. They liked it because it was handy and easily warmed with an open fire.

The next morning they all ate a good breakfast to prepare them for the climb which lay ahead. The trail rose three thousand feet from the wild Whitehorn River and past Emperor Falls. At a place called the Flying Trestle, it crossed a sheer rock face. The place got its name from a road which had been built there by mountaineers. They had drilled holes into the face of the rock and set long, heavy logs in the holes. The logs had been braced, and a wood shelf six feet wide and one hundred feet long had been built on top of them. A small pole railing was on the outside. No one who crossed the Flying Tres-tle ever forgot it! It was safe, but it was no place for a person who was easily frightened. Anyone who looked down could see the churning, rocky Emperor River 1,500 feet below! The trestle had been used for thirty-five years. At last its logs began to rot, and it was blasted away. A new trail ten feet wide was carved the length of the face of the rock. This is the trail the Neighbors had to travel. It was steep, but it was easier on the nerves than the old trestle would have been. The crossing was slow, but they made it safely.

15

The travelers were high in the mountains now, and the nights were freezing cold. Six days after leaving the home ranch, they rode into beautiful alpine meadows. The country was dotted with lakes and closed in on all sides by rugged mountains. It was good caribou country. The group made camp to give Jim a chance to hunt. They stayed a day which was long enough for Jim to kill a large bull caribou.

18

Game was plentiful. They saw wolverine and mountain goats, and there were fresh bear diggings along the trail. In the early part of September they reached Boundary Lake. The group was nine days and seventy miles from the home ranch. Hunters from Slave Lake, Alberta, were camped at the lake, and Hersch liked the company. He decided to make camp to give Jim a chance to try for a mountain goat.

Art spent the first morning shoeing the horses. Eunice baked bread and made the first cake of the trip. The guide from Slave Lake dug out an old map of the Murray River country and traced a copy for the Neighbors. He marked as many trails, rivers, and turn offs as he could remember.

"Don't get tangled up and go down the Wapiti River," he warned. "It'll take you east to Alberta, instead of north."

As it grew dark, Jim and Hersch rode into camp tired and hungry after hunting all day. Jim was pleased and showed the burly head of the goat he had shot.

The Neighbors camped at the lake for a few more days. The third morning they awoke to the first snow of the season. They knew there was one high pass they had to cross, and it looked like the weather was getting bad. They broke camp the next morning. It was September 7, and a bitterly cold wind was blowing down from the high peaks. The snow in the pass was so deep it was hard to see the trail. Even the horses got confused.

Once they were through the pass, they dropped down into heavy timber. It was a jumble of fallen trees, or windfalls as they're called, and rock all covered with snow. They lost the trail and came down the mountain in the wrong place. Halfway to the bottom, a stiff-legged little pack mare fell over a windfall. She landed on her side on top of some fallen trees. Her legs were pointed uphill, and she was about four feet off the ground. The mare could not get up. Hersch, Art, and Jim took the pack off her back so she could roll over. Once her legs were pointed downhill, she slid down the windfall, fell off the bottom and scrambled to her feet. Although cut and skinned in a dozen places, she appeared to be all right and could still carry a pack.

"This is no way to move," Hersch admitted, when they started out again.

Toward evening, they arrived at a meadow near Kakwa Lake. They had been gone from the home ranch for thirteen days, and had come less then one hundred miles. The country they knew was behind them now. Ahead lay more than two hundred miles of wilderness they had never seen. All they had to follow was the guide's old map.

They were tired, hungry, cold, and discouraged. The trip was taking longer than had been expected. Hersch decided to lay over for three days at Kakwa Lake. There good grazing could be found for the horses and they would have time to rest. Jim could also hunt a little more.

Their camp was near a place called Thunder Valley. It got its name from the rumble of snow slides that roared down from the high slopes during the summer. On the second morning as they sat down for breakfast, they heard what sounded like a slide.

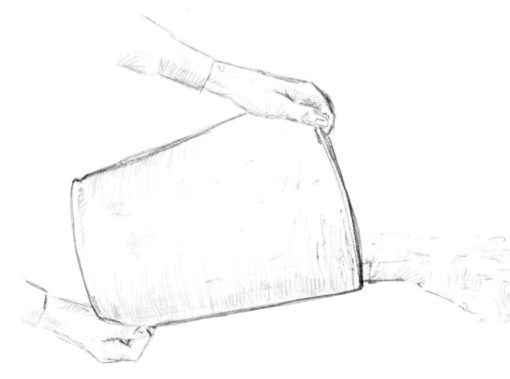

"That's coming from the wrong direction," Art said. He listened a few seconds more. "It wouldn't be our tent burning would it?"

He said it so calmly that everyone thought he was kidding. They lifted the flap of the cook tent and peered out into the morning light. He was right! The tent where he, Jim, and Nod slept was going up in flames!

Nod grabbed a pail and ran to the water hole. Hersch and Jim headed for the burning tent to rescue the guns and bullets. The fire was burning quickly, and the roof was already gone. Nod tried to put out the flames which were shooting up around his father, but he did not have enough water in his pail. All he did was get Jim's sleeping bag wet. Hersch and Jim pulled the gear out, and then started slashing ropes as fast as they could. It was all over in a few minutes. Art and Eunice dragged the remains off to one side, but there wasn't enough left to be of any use. They had been lucky since no one lost any of his gear.

Hersch and Eunice turned their tent over to the three and spent the next few nights in shelters made from spruce boughs. They managed to keep fairly dry in spite of daily rains. As the weather grew worse, the three crowded into the cook tent with Sandy.

Four days later they continued their ride north. After two days they reached Torrens Creek. It was good sheep country, and Hersch decided to make camp for a few days to give Jim time to hunt. This would be his last chance to try for a bighorn sheep. Day after day, there were low clouds, fog, rain and snow. It was poor hunting weather.

On the fourth afternoon, the three men finally got above the fog. The snow cleared, and they found some sheep grazing in a little valley. Jim easily scored one with a full curl to his horns. It was dark by the time they finished dressing it and started down the mountain. The fog made the stormy night seem even darker and the climb was rough. Along with the sheep's head, they were carrying heavy loads of meat. For two hours, they felt their way along the mountainside, stumbling and sliding. It was after midnight as they rode into camp. They were cold and tired, but happy with the result of the day's hunting.

The next morning they broke camp and started out. An hour later, all signs of the trail disappeared. All that could be seen for miles was muskeg swamp and windfalls. There seemed to be no other way to go, so they plunged ahead. One after another, the horses bogged down and had to be pulled free. A pack mare got stuck in a narrow, bottomless creek. All that was holding her up was the pack on her

back. Being wider than the channel of water, the pack was stuck between the banks of the creek.

The men tied one end of a rope to the mare's halter, the other to the saddle horn on Art's horse. Art kept the rope tight so the mare would not sink deeper. Then he reached into the mud and tied a second rope around one of her hind legs, and a third rope to her tail. Art's horse pulled on the halter rope. Jim and Nod pulled on the rope tied to her leg while Sandy, Eunice, and Hersch strained on the other. They were able to lift the mare just enough to get the pack off her back. They gathered their strength, and pulled again. Eunice was sure they would either break her neck or pull off her tail. They pulled some more, and suddenly, the mare was free. It had taken two hours to free her. She seemed all right, so they fastened the pack on her back and set out once again. Even though very tired, they had to keep moving.

Late in the day, they found enough high ground for a camp where there was also some grass for the horses. The weary group crawled into their sleeping bags early that night, but had no more than gone to sleep when a fierce wind began to howl. It was blowing so hard they were afraid it would rip the tents. The stovepipe in the cook tent was rattling, and the lamp that hung on the main pole was swinging back and forth. They got up quickly and

27

checked all the ropes. All seemed secure. Exhausted, they crawled back into their sleeping bags and fell asleep with the storm howling around them.

The next morning the travelers awoke to a strange stillness. An hour before dawn, Sandy peered out from under the tent wall. There were four inches of snow on the ground and more was coming down. They got up and huddled close to each other in the cook tent to eat breakfast. The travelers did not dare waste any more time, so they set out again in spite of the snow. The storm was so bad, Art could hardly find the horses.

"If we ever get out of the bush alive, I'm going to quit ranching," he promised. "I'm going to find a chunk of land, build a nice log house, get me several hens and settle down."

Harder days lay ahead. The country seemed like an endless swamp. The earth was too wet and soft to ride in some places, so they had to lead the horses for miles. The horses got stuck in the muck again and again. Each time, they had to be pulled free. The packs worked loose and had to be tightened, and there were too many windfalls to

count. They had to detour around each one, or cut a new trail. To make matters worse, they were not sure where they were.

"We may not be lost, but we're sure badly confused," Hersch grumbled at supper that night.

"Maybe I only want a little piece of ground, a small cabin, and a few dozen chickens," Art muttered. He was very discouraged, too.

After five days of hard travel they finally got out of the muskeg bog. It was now the latter part of September. For the first time since leaving Boundary Lake, they saw other signs of life. Whoever it was had gone north which was the way Hersch wanted to go, so he followed their trail. It led to a river that flowed north, and they camped there overnight. Seeing the tracks had made everyone feel better.

Ten minutes after leaving camp the next morning, their joy turned to despair. They came to a bog worse than any they had ever crossed. The ground was very shaky. If they climbed one of the little hills, a swamp spruce fifty feet away would sway. There was no way around it, so they started across. The horses sank into muck up to their bellies, and much new trail had to be cut. Sometimes it took four hours to go a mile-and-a-half. The horses were so tired, they would give up and fall over when a windfall halted them.

"One hen is enough!" Art growled as he tried to roll a cigarette when they stopped for lunch. A huge snowflake had fallen on his cigarette paper before he could lick it shut, and he threw it to the ground in disgust. His patience was almost gone.

"I don't need much. I just want to get out of here," he said.

A few hours before dark, they did. They got free of the bog, rode up a ridge and got their first look at Wapiti Lake. This was the spot the guide, they had met back at Boundary Lake, had warned them about. The Wapiti River ran east into Alberta, and that was not the way they wanted to go. They wanted to go north, along the Murray River to the Peace River country. They scouted around, and finally found a good trail alongside a stream. They thought the river might be the Wapiti, but it seemed to be the only way to get through. After about an hour's trail ride, it swung away from the water. Their spirits soared! They were headed for the Murray River at last! This would be the final leg of their journey.

They soon found they were wrong. The trail turned back again to the same stream after a few miles. Hersch decided they would stay on the trail anyway. Since the river seemed to be flowing almost due north, he figured it must be the Murray River. They had already missed the Wapiti.

By now their food supplies were almost gone. The Neighbors had planned for a thirty-day trip, and thirty days had passed. It did not seem possible that they could go hungry in the wilderness. There had been plenty of moose and bear signs while on the mountain trails, but they had seen nothing while traveling in the muskeg for the past ten days. The

34

next morning, Hersch and Jim left camp with their rifles and fishing gear. All around, there was wet snow on the ground and it was cold. Because of their low food supply they knew they had to shoot or catch something.

"We'll bring supper, but I don't know what it will be," Hersch promised.

The men still had not returned by late that afternoon, so Eunice began making a meal using what little they had. She was wondering what to do next, when Art came bounding into the cook tent.

"There's a moose in our camp!" he yelled.

Eunice grabbed her rifle and bolted out of the tent. There, not seventy-five yards from the frying pan, was a young bull moose. It was feeding in the willows at the edge of the timber. She took careful aim and dropped it with one good, clean shot. Art and Nod were still dressing it when Hersch and Jim rode into camp with a pack full of fish and some blue grouse. Supper that night was a real treat. They had stew, fried trout and moose steaks.

Their luck began to change. Late in the afternoon of the next day, they found an empty trapper's cabin on the river bank. From the looks of things, the place had not been used for years. But hanging by a wire from the ridge pole was a ten pound bag of sugar. Although it was wet, it was clean. They set up camp, built a roaring fire to dry themselves, and brewed a huge pail of tea. Then they took turns squeezing drops of sugar syrup into their cups. It was the first sugar they had tasted in many days. Looking around after supper, Nod found the trapper's name and address carved in the wall. Hersch wrote it down so he could repay him for the sugar later.

For the next two days, they rode through more mud and muskeg. It was not as bad as before, but they still were not sure where they were. By evening of the second night, they saw lights twinkling across the muskeg to the north. That had to be the town of East Pine, where the Hart Highway crossed the Murray River. They had followed the right river after all, Hersch thought to himself. He breathed a sigh of relief. Soon they would be in the Peace River country where they planned to winter the horses. In the morning, everyone took baths and put on their last clean clothes. Except for the trapper's old cabin, it had been more than a month since they had seen a house. It was the final day of September as they eagerly set out on the last leg of their journey.

They were still in the muskeg, but seeing the lights the night before had made them all feel better. By noon, they had found a road. It was covered with ice, but anything was better then the muskeg. Eunice huddled deeper into her coat. There had been over thirty days of rain, wind, and snow since they had left the home ranch, and an aching pain had crept into her bones. She knew now how the pioneer women must have felt in the days of the covered wagon.

There were eighteen inches of water on the road, with half-an-inch of ice on top. They slogged along as best they could, but the horses broke through with each step. Finding the road led them to believe they were close to the town whose lights they had seen the night before. There were also colored markers along the road. The markers were the type used in the bush by bulldozer crews exploring for oil. The road they were following wasn't a real road after all. It was just a path slashed through the bush to help the oil crews move their equipment. It went nowhere!

For a minute, Eunice wondered why they had been such fools. Why had they taken on this hardship of the last five weeks? She thought about all the reasons for the trip. If they could do it over again, their decision would probably be the same. They were pioneers at heart.

Eunice was so lost in her thoughts, she almost didn't hear Hersch's call to help prepare lunch. While helping gather firewood, Hersch saw a sign nailed to a tree that made his heart sink. The sign read: "Keep Alberta Green."

He knew where they were at last. It had been the Wapiti River they had followed, instead of the Murray. They were no longer in British Columbia, but in Alberta. If those were not the lights of East Pine they had seen, whose were they?

In their confusion, they had strayed at least one hundred miles off their route. It was late in the season, and the country was rough. They could not hope to retrace their steps.

KEEP
ALBERTA
GREEN

41

"Well, we've moved," Hersch said bitterly as he sat down before the roaring fire. "But it looks like we moved to the wrong place." They camped for the night, tired, discouraged, and lost.

The next day the weary travelers knew they had to keep going no matter what was ahead. Two hours after starting, they found a homesteader's shack with a line of washing hanging in the yard. They greeted such a sign of human life eagerly. The homesteader told them it had been lights from Hinton Trail that they had seen twinkling in the dark the night before. The town was sixteen miles from there. Saying farewell to the homesteader, they continued their journey.

43

Five miles down the road they came to some fenced land and an empty house. It belonged to a farmer who told them they were welcome to use both. They turned their horses out to graze and moved their gear into the old house. Having set up their camp stove, they turned in for the night. It was the first time in two weeks they were able to enjoy a warm, dry place in which to sleep. In the morning, Hersch made a deal with the farmer to leave the horses in the pasture until he could find a place to keep them for the winter. The farmer also agreed to lead them to the town of Hazelmere which was only three miles away. After the farmer's team was hitched to the wagon, the travelers' gear was loaded. Six downcast people plodded along behind the wagon on the early October morning as they traveled the muddy road to Hazelmere.

Hersch found a wintering place for the horses a short distance from Dawson Creek. From there, they headed back to the home ranch traveling first by bus, then by train. On October 7th they arrived at the ranch. It had been forty-three days of a mistaken journey!

When spring came, Hersch and a friend went back to Dawson Creek where they had left the horses. The men drove the horses up the Alaska Highway to mile point one hundred, then west to the Halfway River. They followed the river to the

homestead site along Cypress Creek. It was cold, and there was still deep snow on the ground.

The two men cut enough logs to build a cabin. They worked as fast as they could, but had not completed the cabin by the time Eunice and Sandy arrived. The women had driven a truck filled with furniture to mile point 147. There the furniture was loaded into a wagon pulled by a team of horses and moved through the brush to the site of the home-stead. They were home at last!

Hersch and Eunice still live along Cypress Creek. They own almost five thousand acres of land and have a large herd of horses and cattle. It takes a lot of fence to stake out that much land, and repair-ing what the moose and bear tear down is a con-stant chore. The Neighbors wanted wild country, and they found it. They feel the long, hard move was worth it. If they ever move again, however, both Hersch and Eunice agree they'll wait for a good road and a modern van!

47

Stay on the edge of your seat.

Read:

FROZEN TERROR

DANGER IN THE AIR

MISTAKEN JOURNEY

TRAPPED IN DEVIL'S HOLE

DESPERATE SEARCH

FORTY DAYS LOST

FOUND ALIVE

GRIZZLY!

SURVIVAL TRUE STORIES